The Boy Who Would Grow Up To Be

President
Barack Obama

Boys grow up
to be heroes

Vol. 3

Words by
A.D. Largie

Pictures by
Sabrina Pichardo

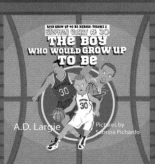
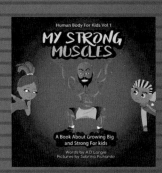

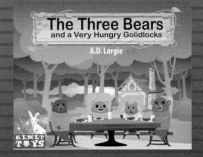

Once upon a time not so long ago a boy was born to a very proud Mama.

His name was Barack Obama.

Barack was different than the other boys because his mom was an American and his father was a KENYAN.

When Barack was 3 years old he felt so sad because his family broke up and he really missed his dad.

Barack's family was very diverse with many kinds of people from Europe, Africa and Asia.

Barack wanted all people to live together in harmony the same way different kinds of people were members of his family.

Barack's favorite sport is basketball he loved playing with his team and he is actually pretty tall.

As a child Barack lived in many places like Hawaii, Washington, & Indonesia.

Then when he got older he moved to New York City to attend Columbia University.

Barack graduated from Columbia University when he grew up because he studied a lot, did his homework and never gave up.

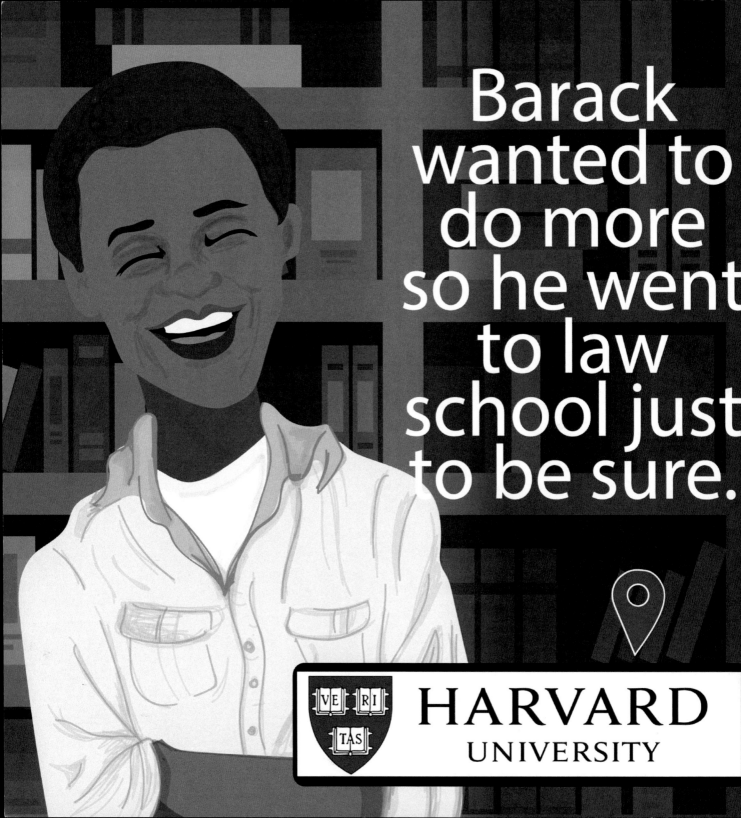

Barack wanted to do more so he went to law school just to be sure.

HARVARD UNIVERSITY

His classmates at Harvard thought he could do more too so they elected him President of the Harvard Law Review.

HARVARD

But his favorite job was as a community Organizer because he believes that people can make their own community better

In Chicago Barack married Michelle Obama, wrote a book and had his two daughters Malia and Sasha.

TIME

Many people liked and trusted **Barack Obama** because he was **FAIR** and treated everyone like a **brother.**

Many important business people and politicians saw what Barack could do. He raised money organized voters and his influence grew.

Barack received support from many people who don't usually like each other.

In 1997 Barack Obama became a United States Senator.

In a few short years Barack Obama was ready to do more and the people of the United States was ready to open the White House door.

In the year 2008 Barack Obama was elected to be the 44th U.S. President his victory was clear and evident.

Wednesday, June 4, 2008

DAILY @ NEWS

2.5 million reader every day

It was the FIRST TIME a non-white man was elected PRESIDENT. Most people were happy because of how the election went.

But some people were angry because they did not want to see the the 1st black president.

ELECTION SPECIAL

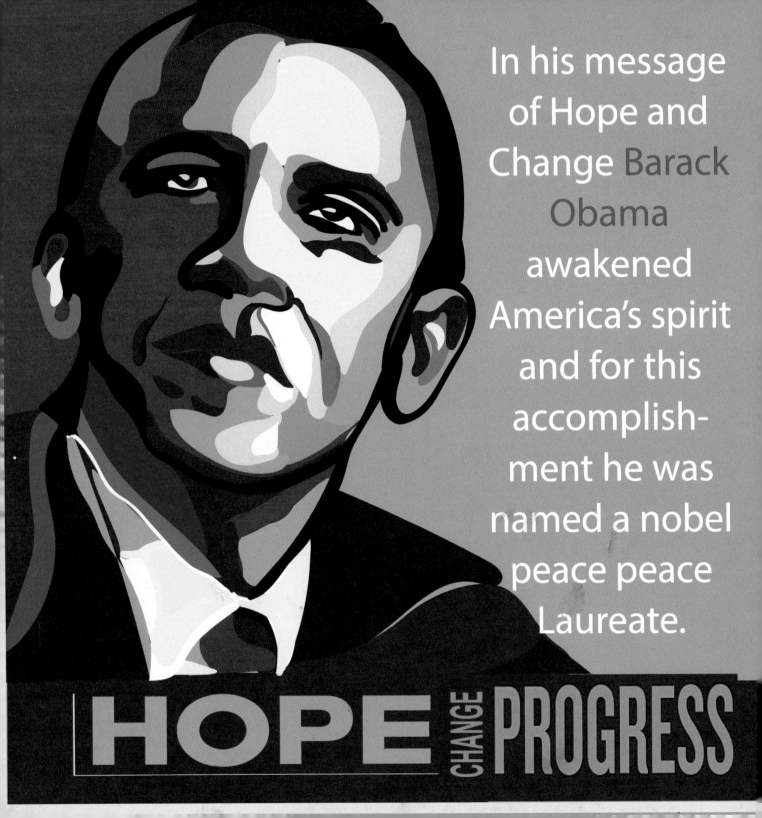

In his message of Hope and Change Barack Obama awakened America's spirit and for this accomplish-ment he was named a nobel peace peace Laureate.

HOPE CHANGE PROGRESS

OBAMA WINS

Barack Obama was elected to be President of the United States twice and it felt so nice.

ELECTIONS 2012

Barack Obama proved that you can can do anything that you believe as long as you hope for the best and focus you can achieve.

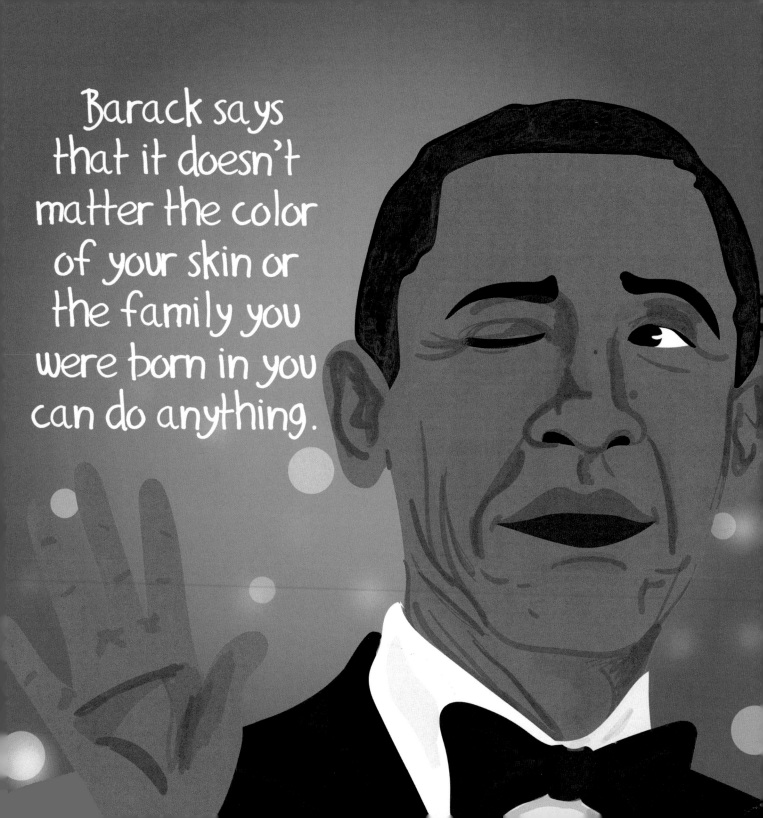

Barack says that it doesn't matter the color of your skin or the family you were born in you can do anything.

www.Amazon.com/author/adlargie

Made in the USA
Monee, IL
09 October 2020